I0479788

This book is for those who are willing to take action, those who seek inspiration, and for those who aspire to achieve financial freedom. It's a story of resilience, perseverance, and determination. Whether you're starting from scratch or looking to take your finances to the next level, this book will inspire you to keep pushing forward and never give up on your dreams.

CONTENTS

INTRODUCTION

Living a life free from financial worries is a dream shared by many people around the world. But for those who come from humble beginnings, this dream can seem like an unattainable fantasy. Growing up in a poor family can be a challenging experience, filled with uncertainty, hardships, and a constant struggle to make ends meet. As a child, I knew all too well the feeling of lacking the means to afford the things I desired.

I was born into a family with limited means, just one brother and two sisters. From a young age, I quickly learned that material possessions were not something we could afford. While other kids were getting the latest gaming consoles or new clothes, I had to make do with what I had. School was my escape from the harsh reality of my financial situation. I was a studious child and focused on my studies, never giving much thought to material possessions.

However, my perspective changed when I moved to a new school at the age of fourteen. It was here that I made new friends who would go out to eat every Friday after school, a tradition that I couldn't afford to participate in. My friends paid for my meals, but the feeling of shame lingered within me. It was during this time that I realized just how dire my family's financial situation was.

To keep track of my finances, I started a record on my computer to log the money I received from my parents each month. To my surprise, the average income I had was a maximum of 10$

per month, which is equivalent to a measly 120$ per year. As a teenager, this was a devastating reality that left me feeling helpless.

To pay for my university tuition fees, I took up a job as a runner inside a restaurant. Eventually, I worked my way up to becoming a waiter, which enabled me to buy new clothes and gaming titles for my console. However, despite my hard work, tuition fees remained a constant struggle. I found myself in a position where I had to pay $2500 to sit my final exams, a daunting sum that seemed impossible to raise.

At that point, I felt lost and didn't know what to do. I prayed for a miracle, and it came in the form of a newfound knowledge of how to modify video game consoles. With nothing to lose, I started advertising my services and soon found myself with a steady stream of customers. The business was successful, and I was able to pay for my tuition fees and have some money left over. I continued to modify consoles on the side while pursuing my studies.

My success with console modifications was a turning point in my life, and it made me realize that anything was possible with the right mindset and determination. I met my wife at university, and together, we shared a passion for entrepreneurship. We both left our 9 to 5 jobs to pursue our dreams and started our own business. I completed my master's degree in computer and communication engineering, and our business began to thrive.

Through this book, I hope to provide readers with a detailed account of my journey, highlighting the obstacles I faced and the strategies I used to overcome them. I believe that my story will inspire others who may be facing similar challenges and show them that it is possible to achieve financial success, no matter how humble your beginnings.

As we explore my journey in the following chapters, I will share my successes, failures, and the lessons I learned along the way. I will provide insights into the strategies that helped me achieve my goals, and how I persevered through difficult times. My story is a testament to the power of determination, hard work, and the willingness to take risks to achieve your dreams.

I believe that this book will not only inspire readers but also provide practical advice and strategies that they can apply in their own.

CHAPTER 1
EARLY LIFE AND EDUCATION

I grew up in a small town, in a poor family with one brother and two sisters. Life was always a challenge for us, and my parents had to work long hours to provide for us. Despite their hard work, we still faced financial constraints and had to live in a small house with just the basic necessities. We did not have many luxuries, and there were many things that we were unable to afford. I often felt left out when my classmates talked about the latest gaming consoles or gadgets that they had received as gifts. This made me realize early on that I had to be resourceful and creative with the limited resources that I had.

My parents always stressed the importance of education and how it was the key to a better future. They encouraged me to work hard and excel in my studies, even though we did not have much money to spare. I knew that if I wanted to achieve my goals and make a better life for myself, I had to take my education seriously.

However, it was not easy to keep up with the expenses that came with studying. With limited resources, I had to find ways to manage my finances and keep track of the little income that I received from my parents. One of the ways I managed my finances was by budgeting my expenses. I created a spreadsheet where I recorded all my expenses and income, and I tried my best to stick to my budget. This helped me to save some money, which I could use to buy some essential school supplies or save up for my future.

Additionally, I often found myself selling some of my old items that I no longer used or needed to get some extra cash. I would sell old clothes, books, and even some of my toys to make some extra money. I learned to be resourceful and creative with my limited resources. I knew that every little bit helped, and I had to take advantage of every opportunity to save money.

However, it was not just financial difficulties that I faced during my childhood. I also had to deal with the pressure of being an excellent student. I felt like I had to prove myself to my classmates and teachers because of my background. I often felt like I was not good enough, and this affected my confidence. However, I did not let this discourage me. I used this pressure as motivation to work harder and smarter.

I had to find creative ways to study and learn with limited resources. I made the most of my local library, which had a good collection of books, magazines, and newspapers. I would often spend hours at the library reading books on various subjects. I borrowed textbooks from my friends and classmates and made notes from them. I also used online resources and educational videos to supplement my learning. I made sure to use my time wisely and study whenever I had the chance.

I also had to sacrifice some leisure time to catch up on my studies, but I knew that this was necessary if I wanted to achieve my goals. I missed out on some fun activities with my friends, but I never felt like I was missing out on anything because I knew that my hard work would pay off.

Despite the challenges that I faced, I remained focused on my studies and was able to excel in my academics. I received scholarships for my outstanding performance and was able to attend a good university. Looking back, I am grateful for the challenges that I faced because they taught me valuable lessons about resilience, resourcefulness, and determination.

Growing up, my parents always emphasized the importance of education. They knew that it was the key to a better future, and they wanted us to have a better life than they did.

SUMMARY:

1.   Resourcefulness and creativity can go a long way in achieving your goals. Don't be discouraged by limited resources; instead, find ways to make the most of what you have.

2.   Budgeting your expenses can help you save money and manage your finances better. Keeping track of your income and expenses can help you make informed decisions and save for your future.

3.   Education is a valuable tool for success, and it is important to take it seriously. Even if you come from a disadvantaged background, hard work and dedication can help you achieve your goals.

4.   Don't let the pressure of proving yourself to others affect your confidence. Use it as motivation to work harder and smarter.

5.   Time management is crucial for success. Sacrificing some leisure time to catch up on studies may be necessary, but it is important to find a balance and not burn out.

6.   Take advantage of available resources, such as libraries, online resources, and educational videos, to supplement your learning.

7.   Finally, be grateful for the challenges that you face, as they

can teach you valuable lessons about resilience, resourcefulness, and determination.

CHAPTER 2
UNIVERSITY LIFE
AND EARLY JOBS

As I stepped onto the sprawling campus of the university, I was hit with a wave of emotion. The campus was bustling with students, each one with their own goals and dreams. It was a stark contrast to the quiet and humble life that I had led up until that point.

But the excitement was short-lived. As I looked around, I realized that I was surrounded by students who seemed to come from much more affluent backgrounds than mine. They dressed in the latest fashions and carried the newest gadgets. I felt a pang of jealousy but refused to let it get to me. I had worked hard to get here, and I was determined to make the most of my opportunity.

My first few weeks at the university were a blur of activity. I attended classes, made new friends, and explored the campus. But as the reality of my situation set in, I knew that I needed to find a job. With tuition fees and living expenses piling up, I had to find a way to support myself financially.

I landed a job as a runner in a local restaurant, where I worked long hours carrying heavy trays of food back and forth. The work was physically demanding, and at times, I was so hungry that my stomach growled loudly. But I didn't have the luxury of taking a break to eat. I had to keep working to make ends meet.

Despite the long hours and exhaustion, I refused to give up. I was determined to work my way through university, and nothing was going to stop me. The money that I earned from my job was barely enough to cover the cost of transportation to the university and tuition fees, leaving me with little left over for other expenses.

I often found myself staring longingly at the food that I was serving to customers, wishing that I could afford to eat there myself. But I knew that I couldn't afford it. So, I learned to make do with what I had, packing a small lunch that I could eat quickly during my breaks.

But as the demands of work and studying piled up, I realized that I needed more income to support myself. So, I took on odd jobs whenever I could find them. I worked as a tutor, a freelance writer, and even took on part-time jobs at a local store. I worked tirelessly, using every spare moment to earn the money that I needed to cover my expenses.

It wasn't easy, but I refused to give up. I was determined to succeed, to prove to myself and to others that I could achieve my dreams. And with hard work and perseverance, I eventually graduated from university with honors.

Looking back on those years, I realize that they were some of the most challenging and rewarding of my life. I learned the value of hard work and perseverance, and I discovered that anything is possible if you are willing to put in the effort. My early struggles shaped me into the person that I am today, and I am grateful for every hardship and challenge that I faced.

SUMMARY:

1.   Don't let your background or financial situation discourage you from pursuing your dreams. You may encounter others who seem to come from more privileged backgrounds, but that doesn't mean you can't achieve your goals.

2.   If you're struggling to make ends meet, consider finding a job or taking on odd jobs to help support yourself financially. Don't be afraid to work hard and take on multiple jobs if needed.

3.   Learn to make do with what you have. It's okay to pack a simple lunch or find other ways to save money. Remember, your focus should be on your education and achieving your goals, not on keeping up with others who may have more resources.

4.   Perseverance is key. Don't give up when faced with challenges or setbacks. Keep pushing yourself and remember that hard work pays off in the end.

5.   Embrace the struggles and challenges you face. They can shape you into a stronger and more resilient person, and you may even discover new strengths and abilities that you didn't know you had.

CHAPTER 3
PASSION FOR GAMING

Growing up in poverty, I found solace in the world of gaming. It was an escape from the harsh realities of my life, a way to lose myself in a world where anything was possible. My love for gaming began at a young age, and it only grew stronger as I got older.

I remember the first time I picked up a controller, I was amazed by the way I could control the character on the screen with just a few simple buttons presses. I quickly became obsessed with video games, spending hours upon hours playing and exploring new worlds.

As I got older, my passion for gaming only intensified. I would spend hours reading gaming magazines, watching videos of the latest gaming titles, and exploring online gaming communities. I was fascinated by the creativity and innovation behind each new title and couldn't wait to get my hands on them.

It wasn't until I landed a job at a DVD and gaming shop that I realized my passion for gaming could become something more than just a hobby. Walking into the shop for the first time, I was in awe of the shelves lined with the latest gaming titles and accessories.

Starting out as a cashier, I quickly worked my way up to a sales associate position. It was here that I discovered my true talent: recommending games to customers based on their interests and playing style. With my deep knowledge and love for gaming, I was able to easily connect with customers who shared my passion for video games and help them find the perfect game to fit their needs.

But it wasn't just the sales aspect of the job that drew me in. I was fascinated by the process of modifying video game consoles and spent countless hours learning everything I could about console modifications. Customers would come to me specifically for console modifications, and I took great pride in helping them achieve the ultimate gaming experience.

Working in the DVD and gaming shop was a dream come true for me. I was surrounded by the latest gaming consoles, titles, and accessories, and I spent my breaks trying out new games and exploring new worlds. It was a job that gave me a sense of fulfillment and purpose that I had never experienced before.

But my passion for gaming wasn't just limited to my job. It was a driving force in my life, and I knew that I wanted to pursue a career in the gaming industry. The knowledge and experience I gained working at the DVD and gaming shop were invaluable, and I was confident that I was on the right path towards achieving my goals.

My passion for gaming has played a significant role in shaping who I am today. It has given me a sense of direction and purpose, and it has allowed me to connect with others who share my love for video games. While my childhood may have been marked by poverty and struggle, my passion for gaming provided me with a sense of escape and hope.

In conclusion, my passion for gaming has been a constant in my life, driving me to pursue my dreams and excel in my career. It has given me a sense of fulfillment and purpose and has allowed me to connect with others who share my love for video games. Working at the DVD and gaming shop was a pivotal moment in my life, and I will always be grateful for the experiences and opportunities it provided me.

SUMMARY:

1.   Embrace your passions and find solace in the things that bring you joy.

2.   Pursue opportunities to learn and grow in areas that interest you.

3.   Use your expertise and knowledge to connect with others who share your passion.

4.   Recognize the value in sharing your passions with others, whether it's through recommending games or helping with console modifications.

5.   Take pride in your work and find fulfillment in the sense of purpose it provides.

6.   Use your passions to drive you towards achieving your goals and pursuing your dreams.

7.   Remember the role that your passions have played in shaping who you are and the opportunities they can bring.

CHAPTER 4
RELATIONSHIP
AND MARRIAGE

Relationships can be complex and are influenced by various factors, such as family background, social norms, personal beliefs, and life experiences. In this chapter, I will discuss my relationship with my wife and how it evolved over the course of ten years.

Our love story began during our university years where we were both pursuing degrees in different fields. We met through mutual friends and gradually got to know each other better. Our personalities complemented each other, and we shared many common interests, including our passion for gaming. We spent a lot of time together, whether it was studying, playing video games, or just hanging out.

As our relationship progressed, we faced some challenges that tested our commitment to each other. One of the biggest obstacles was our financial situation. We both came from humble backgrounds and had to work part-time jobs to support ourselves while studying. We could not afford to get married earlier because we did not have enough savings or financial stability to support a family.

Despite the financial challenges, we remained committed to each other and continued to build our relationship. We had a shared vision of our future and worked towards it, even though it seemed daunting at times. We knew that we wanted to start our own business someday and that we needed to save enough money to make it a reality.

As we approached the end of our university years, we started to think seriously about our future. We realized that the traditional 9-5 job was not the only option available to us, and that we could create our own path as entrepreneurs. We saw the potential in starting our own business and building something that we could call our own.

The transition from a 9-5 job to entrepreneurship was not an easy one. We had to overcome our fears and doubts and take calculated risks. We had to learn new skills and techniques to build and grow our business. We had to make sacrifices and work harder than ever before.

But it was all worth it. Our shared vision and determination kept us motivated, and we worked together to overcome the challenges that came our way. Our relationship grew stronger as we faced new challenges and celebrated our successes together.

One of the things that helped us strengthen our relationship was the fact that we both shared a passion for gaming. We would spend hours playing video games together, laughing, and having fun. It was a great way to unwind and forget about the stress of work and other responsibilities. Our mutual love for gaming also allowed us to bond over shared interests, and we would often discuss different games and strategies together.

Another thing that helped us build our relationship was our shared commitment to personal growth and development. We both knew that we wanted to achieve great things in life, and we were willing to work hard to make those dreams a reality. We supported each other through our successes and failures, and we always believed in each other's potential.

Despite the many challenges we faced, our relationship remained strong, and we eventually got married after ten years of being together. It was a beautiful day filled with love, laughter, and joy. We exchanged vows, promising to love and support each other through thick and thin, for better or for worse.

Marriage brought new challenges and opportunities for growth. We had to learn to navigate each other's quirks and habits, and we had to make compromises and sacrifices to keep our relationship strong. We had to communicate more effectively, and we had to learn to be more patient and understanding.

One of the biggest challenges we faced after getting married was navigating our new roles as partners and learning to make compromises and sacrifices for each other. We had to communicate more effectively, and we had to learn to be more patient and understanding. We also had to learn how to manage our finances together and plan for our future as a couple.

Throughout our journey, gaming remained an important part of our relationship. We continued to play video games together and found that it was a great way to unwind and spend quality time with each other. It allowed us to bond over shared interests and provided a fun escape from the stresses of daily life.

In conclusion, our relationship and marriage have taught us the importance of communication, compromise, and shared vision. We learned that working together towards a common goal, whether it be personal or professional, can be the key to success. It's important to nurture our relationships with care and attention and to support each other through the challenges that life may bring.

SUMMARY:

1.   Shared interests can be a great way to bond with your partner and spend quality time together. Find activities that you both enjoy doing and make time for them regularly.

2.   It's important to have a shared vision for your future and work towards it together. Setting goals and working towards them as a team can strengthen your relationship and give you a sense of purpose.

3.   Communication is key to a healthy relationship. Make sure you communicate openly and honestly with your partner, even about difficult topics. Learn to listen to each other's perspectives and find ways to resolve conflicts.

4.   Marriage and long-term relationships require compromise and sacrifice. You need to be willing to make adjustments to accommodate your partner's needs and preferences, and they should do the same for you.

5.   Remember to nurture your relationship with care and attention. Make time for each other and prioritize your relationship, even when life gets busy. Celebrate your successes together and support each other through the challenges that may arise.

CHAPTER 5
ENTREPRENEURSHIP

Entrepreneurship is a challenging but rewarding journey that requires a holistic approach. Not only does it require taking risks and working hard, but it also necessitates financial literacy, personal development, and a commitment to positive habits. The books "Rich Dad Poor Dad" and "The Richest Man in Babylon" have been great sources of inspiration for entrepreneurs seeking financial education and wealth-building strategies. "Atomic Habits" emphasizes the importance of establishing positive habits to achieve long-term success. Combining these principles with personal experience, success in business requires a clear understanding of finances, achievable goals, and positive habits.

The road to success is never smooth, as experienced by a gaming console and modification service provider. Challenges such as limited resources and competition can be overcome through resourcefulness, creativity, exceptional customer service, and building a strong team. Entrepreneurship taught valuable lessons about persistence, delegation, and being passionate about one's work. While not for everyone, taking the risk and staying focused on achieving dreams can be immensely fulfilling and rewarding.

When I first started my business, I had no idea what I was doing. I had some experience with gaming consoles and modification services, but I had no business background or experience. However, I was determined to succeed, and I was willing to put in the hard work to make it happen.

One of the biggest challenges I faced was limited resources. I didn't have a lot of money to invest in my business, so I had to be resourceful and creative. I started by posting ads on websites offering modification services for gaming consoles. I focused on providing high-quality services and building a strong reputation in the market.

Eventually, my business started to grow, and I was able to invest in new equipment and technologies to improve my services. This helped me attract more customers and expand my business. I also started to hire skilled technicians and an accountant to manage the finances, which helped me focus on growing the business.

Another challenge I faced was competition. The market for gaming consoles and modification services was highly competitive, and I had to find ways to stand out from my competitors. I did this by focusing on providing exceptional customer service and being passionate about my work. I always put my customers first, and this helped me build a loyal customer base.

As my business grew, I met my wife, who shared the same passion for gaming as me. Together, we came up with a plan to expand our business by selling gaming consoles and accessories alongside the modification services we provide. This was a significant milestone for our business as it allowed us to offer a broader range of products and services, which helped us reach a wider customer base.

We continued to research and keep up with the latest gaming trends, which helped us stay ahead of our competitors. We invested in marketing strategies, such as social media and email marketing, to attract new customers. We also kept a close eye on our finances and worked closely with our accountant to manage our expenses effectively.

The experience of entrepreneurship taught me valuable lessons about business and life. I learned the importance of being passionate about my work, being persistent, and never giving up. I also learned the importance of delegation, and how building a team can help you achieve your goals.

Entrepreneurship is not for everyone, but for those who are willing to take the risk, it can be a fulfilling and rewarding experience. If you are thinking about starting your own business, my advice would be to do your research, be passionate about your work, and be prepared to work hard. It won't be easy, but if you stay focused and dedicated, you can achieve your dreams.

In conclusion, entrepreneurship is a journey that requires hard work, dedication, and perseverance. It's not for the faint of heart, but for those who are willing to take the risk, the rewards can be immense. I am proud of what my wife and I have accomplished, and I look forward to the future with excitement and optimism.

SUMMARY:

1.   Take a holistic approach to entrepreneurship. To be successful, it's not just about taking risks and working hard, but also about financial literacy, personal development, and positive habits.

2.   Educate yourself about finances and wealth-building strategies. Books like "Rich Dad Poor Dad" and "The Richest Man in Babylon" can be great sources of inspiration.

3.   Establish positive habits to achieve long-term success. "Atomic Habits" is a book that emphasizes the importance of positive habits in achieving success.

4.   Overcome challenges through resourcefulness, creativity, exceptional customer service, and building a strong team.

5.   Be passionate about your work and be willing to put in the hard work to make your dreams a reality.

6.   Focus on providing exceptional customer service to build a loyal customer base.

7.   Research and keep up with the latest trends in your industry to stay ahead of your competitors.

8.   Work closely with an accountant to manage your finances

effectively.

9.   Never give up and stay persistent in pursuing your goals.

10.   Entrepreneurship is not for everyone, but for those who are willing to take the risk, it can be a fulfilling and rewarding experience.

CHAPTER 6
TRANSITIONING FROM 9-5 TO ENTREPRENEURSHIP

Transitioning from a stable, 9-5 job to entrepreneurship is an exciting, yet daunting experience that requires courage, patience, and a willingness to take risks. This was the reality my wife and I faced when we decided to pursue our passions in technology and entrepreneurship.

As we delved into the process of starting our own business, we realized that it would require extensive research and planning. We spent countless hours assessing our strengths, weaknesses, interests, and skillset to identify the best business opportunities that would allow us to achieve our goals. It was a rigorous process that demanded a deep understanding of ourselves and the market we wanted to enter.

Once we identified the right opportunity, we had to develop a solid business plan that would guide our operations. We meticulously outlined our product offerings, pricing, marketing strategies, and financial projections to ensure that we had a clear roadmap for success.

But the road to success was not without its challenges. The most significant challenge we faced was securing funding for our business. We explored various options, such as loans, grants, and personal investments, and were fortunate enough to secure funding from a local business incubator. It provided us with the initial capital we needed to get our business off the ground.

As we embarked on this new journey, we quickly learned that discipline, focus, and persistence were essential ingredients for success. We had to invest in our personal development and learn new skills to provide the best possible service to our customers. We also had to be patient and persistent, knowing that building a successful business takes time and effort.

One of the critical factors that contributed to our success was our ability to be resourceful and creative. We looked for unique ways to differentiate ourselves from our competitors, such as offering personalized services and establishing a strong brand identity. We also listened to our customers' feedback and made changes to our products and services based on their needs and preferences.

As our business grew, we faced new challenges that tested our adaptability and willingness to change. We had to manage our cash flow, deal with difficult customers, and scale our operations to meet demand. It was a learning experience that taught us the value of being open-minded and flexible in a rapidly evolving tech industry.

Through it all, we never lost sight of the importance of being passionate about our work and taking calculated risks to achieve success. It was our passion for technology and entrepreneurship that drove us to take the leap of faith and start our own business. It was also our willingness to take calculated risks that enabled us to turn our passion into a thriving business.

In conclusion, transitioning from a traditional 9-5 job to entrepreneurship is not for the faint of heart. It requires careful planning, discipline, focus, and a willingness to take risks. But for those who are willing to take the leap of faith, the rewards can be substantial. For my wife and me, starting our own business was a significant turning point in our lives, and we encourage others to follow their passions, take risks, and create a business that aligns with their interests and skillset. The journey may be challenging, but the rewards are well worth it.

SUMMARY:

1.   Be prepared for the challenges of transitioning from a stable 9-5 job to entrepreneurship. It requires courage, patience, and a willingness to take risks.

2.   Spend time assessing your strengths, weaknesses, interests, and skillset to identify the best business opportunities that align with your goals.

3.   Develop a solid business plan that outlines your product offerings, pricing, marketing strategies, and financial projections to provide a clear roadmap for success.

4.   Securing funding for your business can be challenging, but exploring various options, such as loans, grants, and personal investments, can help.

5.   Discipline, focus, and persistence are essential ingredients for success. Invest in your personal development, learn new skills, and be patient and persistent.

6.   Be resourceful and creative. Look for unique ways to differentiate yourself from your competitors and listen to your customers' feedback.

7.   Be open-minded and flexible to change. Manage your cash flow, deal with difficult customers, and scale your operations to

meet demand.

8.   Never lose sight of the importance of being passionate about your work and taking calculated risks to achieve success. Starting your own business can be a significant turning point in your life, and the rewards are well worth the journey.

CHAPTER 7
CHALLENGES IN
STARTING A BUSINESS

Starting my own business had always been a dream of mine. I was passionate about entrepreneurship and the idea of creating something from scratch that could change people's lives. After years of talking about it, I finally decided to take the leap with my wife by my side. We had a solid business plan, a clear vision, and a lot of determination. However, the road ahead was full of challenges that tested us both personally and professionally.

The first hurdle we faced was managing our finances. As someone who had always been responsible with money, I was shocked to learn that running a business was a whole different ballgame. The income was unpredictable, and I had to learn how to budget my money carefully, plan for unexpected expenses, and manage my cash flow. It was daunting, but it taught me valuable lessons about financial management that I still use to this day.

Marketing our business was another significant challenge that I had to overcome. Despite having a great product, getting the word out was a struggle. I tried various marketing techniques, from social media to email marketing to advertising, but nothing seemed to work. It was frustrating, and I started to doubt myself. But I knew that giving up was not an option, so I kept pushing forward, determined to find a solution.

During this period, there were many ups and downs. Some days, I felt like I was making real progress, while others felt like I was taking one step forward and two steps back. It was an emotional rollercoaster, but I learned to stay focused on my goals and believe that my hard work would pay off in the end.

One of the most significant lessons I learned during this journey was the importance of perseverance. Starting a business is not easy, and there were times when it felt like everything was working against me. But I kept pushing forward, even when things were tough. I had to stay focused on my goals and believe that my hard work would pay off in the end.

Another lesson I learned was the importance of adaptability. As I encountered obstacles and setbacks, I had to be willing to change my approach and try new things. I couldn't be rigid in my thinking or my strategies; I had to be open to new ideas and willing to pivot when necessary. This adaptability allowed me to overcome many obstacles and ultimately build a successful business.

It wasn't just the financial and marketing challenges that tested me. I also had to balance work and family life, which was a constant struggle. There were times when I felt like I was neglecting my family in pursuit of my dream, but I had to remind myself that it was all for a greater purpose. I also had to deal with the fear of failure and the pressure to succeed. It was a lot to handle, but I relied on my wife and family for support and found strength in my passion.

Despite all the challenges, I never lost sight of my goal. I had a clear vision of what I wanted to achieve, and I was willing to do whatever it took to get there. It was a long and difficult journey, but in the end, it was worth it. I built a successful business that I am proud of, and I learned a lot about myself in the process.

Starting a business is not for the faint of heart, but for those willing to take the leap, the rewards can be significant. It takes hard work, perseverance, adaptability, and a willingness to learn from mistakes. But with the right mindset and determination, anyone can overcome the challenges and build a business that they can be proud of. My journey was full of obstacles, but it was also full of valuable lessons that have made me a better entrepreneur and person.

SUMMARY:

1.   Be willing to adapt: Starting a business is full of unexpected challenges, and it's important to be willing to change your approach and try new things. Don't be afraid to pivot if something isn't working.

2.   Persevere through tough times: There will be ups and downs, but it's important to stay focused on your goals and keep pushing forward. Believe that your hard work will pay off in the end.

3.   Manage your finances carefully: Running a business requires careful budgeting and planning, especially since income can be less predictable than in traditional jobs. Make sure you have enough money on hand to pay bills and invest in the business.

4.   Don't give up: Starting a business is not easy, but it can be incredibly rewarding. Don't let fear of failure or doubt stop you from pursuing your dreams. Keep pushing forward and stay on the course.

5.   Find support in others: Starting a business can be a lonely journey, but it's important to find support in others. Whether it's a business partner, mentor, or supportive family and friends, having a support system can make all the difference.

CHAPTER 8
STRATEGIES FOR
GROWTH

As we began to offer more services and expand our business, we encountered many challenges along the way. One of the biggest challenges we faced was the need to constantly innovate and offer something unique to our customers. The gaming industry is constantly evolving, and it was important for us to keep up with the latest trends and developments to stay relevant.

To achieve this, we spent countless hours researching and attending industry events to keep up with the latest developments in the gaming industry. We also spent time networking with other businesses in the industry to share ideas and best practices. This helped us to develop new services and products that were innovative and unique, which helped to attract and retain customers.

Another challenge we faced was the need to market our business effectively. In order to attract new customers, we needed to be visible and accessible to them. We used social media, online advertising, and word-of-mouth marketing to reach potential customers. We also developed partnerships with other businesses in the gaming industry, such as video game retailers and online gaming communities, which helped us to increase our exposure and reach more customers.

In addition to expanding our services and marketing our business effectively, we also needed to invest in our business to support our growth. This meant taking calculated risks, such as investing in new equipment and technology, and even opening a physical store. While these investments were significant, they ultimately helped us to attract more customers and grow our business.

However, with growth came new challenges. One of the most significant challenges we faced was hiring and training staff to keep up with the increasing demand for our services. We needed to ensure that our staff was properly trained and equipped to provide quality services to our customers. We also needed to make sure that our customers were satisfied with our work, and that we were able to deliver our services on time and on budget.

To overcome this challenge, we took the necessary steps to train our staff and ensure that they had the skills and knowledge needed to provide quality services. We also implemented quality control measures to ensure that our customers received the best services possible. This helped us to maintain our reputation for quality and reliability, which ultimately helped to attract and retain customers.

Throughout our journey, we learned many valuable lessons about growing a business. We learned that it was important to be adaptable and willing to change strategies as needed. We also learned the importance of listening to our customers and taking their feedback into consideration when developing new services and products. Above all, we learned that it takes dedication, hard work, and a willingness to take calculated risks to grow a successful business.

Our experiences and lessons learned are shared in Chapter 8 to help aspiring entrepreneurs and business owners achieve their goals and grow their businesses. By sharing our story and insights, we hope to inspire others to take the leap and pursue their dreams of starting and growing their own businesses.

SUMMARY:

1.   Keep up with industry trends: The gaming industry is constantly evolving, and it's important to stay up to date with the latest trends and developments. This can be done by attending industry events, networking with other businesses, and researching new technologies.

2.   Market effectively: In order to attract new customers, it's important to be visible and accessible. Use social media, online advertising, and word-of-mouth marketing to reach potential customers. Consider developing partnerships with other businesses in the industry to increase exposure and reach more customers.

3.   Invest in your business: Growing a business requires taking calculated risks, such as investing in new equipment and technology. Consider opening a physical store to attract more customers. Remember that investments may be significant, but they can help attract more customers and grow the business.

4.   Train and equip your staff: As the business grows, it's important to ensure that staff is properly trained and equipped to provide quality services. Implement quality control measures to ensure customers receive the best services possible.

5.   Be adaptable and listen to customers: It's important to be adaptable and willing to change strategies as needed. Listen to customers and take their feedback into consideration when

developing new services and products.

6.   Dedication, hard work, and willingness to take risks: Growing a successful business takes dedication, hard work, and a willingness to take calculated risks. Remember that setbacks and challenges are a natural part of the journey, but they can be overcome with persistence and determination.

CHAPTER 9
REACHING ONE
MILLION DOLLARS

Chapter 9 of my book is a testament to the power of hard work, dedication, and persistence. Achieving financial freedom was a goal that I had been working towards for years, and it was a milestone that changed my life forever. The chapter is an account of the journey that led me to reach one million dollars and the lessons that I learned along the way.

When I started writing my book, I never thought it would lead me to financial freedom. I saw it as a way to share my knowledge and experiences with others and generate some extra income on the side. However, as I started promoting my book, I realized that there was a much bigger demand for it than I had anticipated. The response was overwhelming, and it gave me the boost that I needed to keep pushing forward.

I set a modest goal of selling 10,000 copies, but it quickly became apparent that I had underestimated the potential of my book. People from all over the world were buying it, and it was selling like hotcakes. I was amazed and grateful for the success that I had achieved. Selling over 200,000 copies was a significant accomplishment, but it was the financial freedom that it gave me that was truly life changing.

Reaching one million dollars was an incredible feeling. It was a validation of all the hard work, dedication, and sacrifices that I had made over the years. However, it wasn't just about the money. It was also about the personal satisfaction and sense of accomplishment that came with achieving a goal that I had set for myself.

One of the most critical lessons that I learned was the importance of having a clear vision and strategy for achieving financial freedom. It's not just about making money; it's about having a plan for how you're going to achieve your goals. I spent a lot of time researching and developing my strategy, and it paid off in the end.

Staying disciplined and focused was another critical factor in achieving financial freedom. It was tempting to take shortcuts or deviate from the plan at times, but I knew that I had to stay on track if I wanted to achieve my goal. It was a challenging journey, but it was one that I was willing to make sacrifices for.

Throughout the chapter, I emphasize the importance of continuously learning and improving. The world is constantly changing, and it's essential to stay informed about market trends and opportunities. Investing in education, acquiring new skills, and staying up to date with industry developments are all essential to achieving long-term success.

I also highlight the importance of having a support system in place. Achieving financial freedom was not something that I could have done alone. It required the support of my loved ones, including my family, friends, colleagues, and my wife, who provided me with the encouragement and motivation that I needed to keep going. It was a team effort, and I'm grateful for everyone who played a role in helping me achieve my goal.

In conclusion, Chapter 9 of my book is a celebration of the power of hard work, dedication, and persistence. Achieving financial freedom was a significant milestone in my life, but it was just the beginning. It opened new opportunities and allowed me to pursue other interests and passions. It's a chapter in my life that I will always look back on with pride and gratitude. If there's one thing that I hope readers take away from this chapter, it's the importance of having a clear vision and strategy, staying disciplined and focused, continuously learning and improving, and having a support system in place. These are the keys to achieving success in any endeavor.

SUMMARY:

1.   Set clear goals: Having a clear vision and strategy for achieving financial freedom is important to staying on track and executing a plan.

2.   Work hard: Achieving financial freedom requires hard work, dedication, and sacrifice.

3.   Stay focused: It's important to stay disciplined and focused on executing your plan, even when it's tempting to take shortcuts or deviate from the plan.

4.   Believe in yourself: It's important to have confidence in your abilities and believe in yourself, even when faced with challenges or setbacks.

5.   Invest in education: Continuous learning and improvement are essential to maintaining financial freedom, as the world is constantly evolving.

6.   Be willing to take risks: Financial freedom often requires taking calculated risks, such as starting a business or investing in the stock market.

7.   Seek support from loved ones: Achieving financial freedom is a team effort, and having the support of family, friends, and colleagues can make all the difference.

8.   Pursue your passions: Achieving financial freedom can open new opportunities and allow you to pursue other interests and passions.

9.   Don't get complacent: Once you achieve financial freedom, it's important to continue learning, improving, and staying informed about industry developments to maintain long-term success.

10.   Appreciate your accomplishments: Achieving financial freedom is a significant milestone, and it's important to take the time to reflect on your accomplishments and feel a sense of pride and gratitude for what you've achieved.

CHAPTER 10
REFLECTION AND
GRATITUDE

As I reflect on my journey towards financial freedom, I am reminded of the many challenges, obstacles, and triumphs that I have experienced along the way. I realize that my journey has not only been about achieving financial independence but also about personal growth, self-discovery, and the pursuit of happiness.

One of the most significant lessons that I have learned on my journey is the importance of gratitude. I have come to realize that gratitude is not just a feeling of appreciation or thankfulness towards others; it's also a powerful tool for personal growth and well-being. When we express gratitude, we shift our focus from what we lack to what we have, and we open ourselves up to new opportunities and experiences.

I emphasize the importance of expressing gratitude towards our family, friends, mentors, and customers. They have played an instrumental role in our journey, supporting us through the ups and downs and providing us with guidance and encouragement when we needed it the most.

But expressing gratitude is not just about acknowledging

others; it's also about recognizing and appreciating our own accomplishments and strengths. As I reflect on my journey, I am proud of the hard work, determination, and resilience that my wife and I have demonstrated. We have faced many challenges, but we never gave up, and we always found a way to overcome them. By recognizing our own strengths and accomplishments, we can build confidence and self-esteem, which are essential for personal growth and success.

Another critical lesson that I have learned on my journey is the importance of reflection. Reflection is the process of examining our thoughts, feelings, and experiences, and using that knowledge to inform our future decisions and actions. By reflecting on our journey, we gain a deeper understanding of ourselves and the world around us, which can help us to identify our strengths, weaknesses, and areas for improvement.

I encourage readers to reflect on their own journey towards financial independence or any other goal they are pursuing. By doing so, they can gain valuable insights into their own strengths, weaknesses, and personal growth. They can also use this knowledge to set new goals and take actions that align with their values, interests, and aspirations.

As I conclude my journey towards financial freedom, I am reminded that success is not just about achieving our goals but also about the journey itself. Our journey is an ongoing process of growth and self-discovery, and it requires us to remain humble, grateful, and reflective.

By remaining humble, we acknowledge that our success is not just about our own efforts but also about the support, guidance, and opportunities that others have provided us with. By remaining grateful, we recognize the abundance and blessings in our lives, which can help us to cultivate a positive and optimistic mindset. By remaining reflective, we gain valuable insights into our own journey, which can help us to make better decisions and achieve our goals more effectively.

In conclusion, chapter 10 is not just the end of my journey towards financial freedom, but also the beginning of a new phase in my life. It's a phase of continued growth, self-discovery, and the pursuit of happiness. My hope is that readers find inspiration and guidance in my story, and that they use it to inform their own journey towards personal and financial success. Remember that success is not just a destination; it's an ongoing journey of growth and self-discovery, and it's up to us to make the most of it.

SUMMARY:

1.   Recognize that success is a journey, not a destination: Success is not something that can be achieved overnight. It's a journey that requires time, effort, and commitment.

2.   Be proud of your accomplishments but remain committed to growth and improvement: Celebrate your achievements, but don't let them limit your potential for growth and improvement.

3.   Remember where you came from and acknowledge the lessons you've learned along the way: Don't forget your roots and the lessons you've learned from your past experiences. They can provide valuable insights into your future.

4.   Practice gratitude and recognize the role of others in your success: Show appreciation to those who have helped you along the way and practice gratitude for your blessings.

5.   Reflect on your journey to gain valuable insights for the future: Take time to reflect on your past experiences and learn from them to improve your future.

6.   Be willing to take risks in pursuit of your goals: Success often requires taking calculated risks. Don't be afraid to step out of your comfort zone and pursue your goals.

7.   Stay humble and avoid becoming too caught up in your

own success: Success can be fleeting if you become too caught up in your own achievements. Stay grounded and humble.

8.   Don't let setbacks or failures discourage you; they are opportunities for learning and growth: Everyone experiences setbacks and failures along the way. Use them as opportunities for learning and growth.

9.   Stay optimistic and focused on achieving your goals, even in the face of challenges: A positive mindset can help you overcome challenges and stay focused on achieving your goals.

CONCLUSION

In conclusion, this book has taken us on a journey of self-discovery, growth, and transformation. We have learned the power of perseverance, the importance of having a clear vision for our lives, and the benefits of taking calculated risks. Moreover, we have developed a growth mindset that has allowed us to turn failures and setbacks into opportunities for learning and growth.

Through our story, we hope to inspire and motivate our readers to believe in themselves and stay committed to their goals. We want them to know that they're not alone in their struggles, and that it's possible to overcome challenges and achieve great things. We also want to emphasize the importance of never giving up on our dreams, even when the road seems long and difficult.

In essence, this book is a reminder that anything is possible if we believe in ourselves and stay committed to our goals. It's a testament to the human spirit and the power of resilience. We hope that our story has enriched your life with knowledge, emotions, and words that will remain with you long after you've finished reading. We're grateful for the opportunity to share our journey with you, and we hope that it has made a positive impact on your life.

In addition to the lessons we've learned, we also want to acknowledge the people who have helped us along the way. We wouldn't be where we are today without the support, guidance, and mentorship of others. We've had friends and family who have cheered us on during the tough times, teachers and mentors who have challenged us to grow and learn, and colleagues and peers who have collaborated with us to achieve our goals. We're grateful for all of these individuals, and we encourage you to seek out similar sources of support in your own life.

It's also important to recognize that our journey is ongoing. We haven't reached some final destination or achieved some ultimate goal. Instead, we continue to face new challenges and opportunities every day. We're constantly learning, growing, and evolving, and we recognize that this process will continue for the rest of our lives.

As you continue your own journey, we encourage you to stay curious, stay open-minded, and stay committed to your goals. Keep seeking out new experiences, new perspectives, and new ways of thinking. Surround yourself with people who uplift and inspire you, and never be afraid to ask for help when you need it.

We also want to emphasize the importance of taking care of yourself along the way. It's easy to get caught up in the hustle and bustle of daily life, and to neglect your physical, emotional, and spiritual well-being. But taking care of yourself is essential if you want to achieve long-term success and fulfillment. Make time for rest and relaxation, prioritize healthy habits like exercise and good nutrition, and invest in your own personal growth and development.

In conclusion, we hope that our journey has inspired you to believe in yourself and to stay committed to your own goals and dreams. We hope that the lessons we've learned can help you navigate the challenges and setbacks that you'll inevitably face along the way. And we hope that you'll always remember that anything is possible if you stay focused, stay persistent, and stay true to yourself. Thank you for taking the time to read our story, and we wish you all the best on your own journey.

THE CLOSING STATEMENT AND FUTURE UPDATES

I want to take a moment to express my gratitude to you, the readers, for joining me on this journey. It's been an honor to share my story with you and to offer advice and insights that I hope will help you on your own journey to success.

I know that reading a book like this takes time and effort, and I appreciate the investment that you've made in yourself by reading it. I hope that you've found it to be a valuable resource and that it has given you the inspiration and motivation you need to achieve your own goals.

If you have any feedback or comments about the book, please don't hesitate to reach out to me at "rhassoun@aswakouna.com". I would love to hear from you and to learn more about your own journey.

Also, I want to let you know that an updated version of this book will be available soon, and you can find it at "www.aswakouna.com/Bookupdates" (the link will be available when the new version is uploaded). Be sure to check back regularly for new content and insights that can help you on your path to success.

Finally, I want to tease a new book that I'm currently working on, which will delve deeper into my journey from 1 million to 1 billion. I'm excited to share even more insights and advice with you, and I hope that you'll stay tuned for its release.

Once again, thank you for taking the time to read this book, and I wish you all the best on your journey to success.

SUMMARY

Chapter 1: Set Clear Goals

- Set specific, measurable, achievable, relevant, and time-bound goals.
- Break larger goals down into smaller, more manageable steps.
- Write down your goals and review them regularly.

Chapter 2: Build a Strong Mindset

- Cultivate a growth mindset and believe in your ability to learn and improve.
- Develop resilience to overcome setbacks and challenges.
- Practice mindfulness to stay present and focused on the task at hand.

Chapter 3: Take Consistent Action

- Consistency is key to achieving long-term success.
- Create habits and routines that support your goals.
- Focus on progress, not perfection.

Chapter 4: Embrace Failure

- Failure is an inevitable part of the learning process.
- View failures as opportunities for growth and learning.

- Take calculated risks and learn from both successes and failures.

Chapter 5: Learn from Others

- Seek out mentors and role models who can provide guidance and support.
- Network and collaborate with others in your field.
- Read books, attend conferences, and take courses to learn new skills and stay up to date on industry trends.

Chapter 6: Take Care of Yourself

- Prioritize self-care, including exercise, healthy eating, and getting enough rest.
- Manage stress and avoid burnout by setting boundaries and practicing mindfulness.
- Focus on your overall well-being, not just your professional goals.

Chapter 7: Stay Focused

- Eliminate distractions and prioritize your most important tasks.
- Use time-management techniques, such as the Pomodoro method, to maximize productivity.
- Stay motivated by keeping your goals in mind and celebrating small wins along the way.

Chapter 8: Embrace Change

- Change is inevitable, and it can be a source of growth and opportunity.

- Develop a mindset of flexibility and adaptability.
- Embrace new challenges and seek out opportunities for personal and professional growth.

Chapter 9: Build Strong Relationships

- Develop strong connections with colleagues, clients, and other professionals in your field.
- Practice active listening and empathy to build trust and rapport.
- Invest time and effort into maintaining relationships and building new ones.

Chapter 10: Keep Learning and Growing

- Commit to lifelong learning and personal growth.
- Seek out new challenges and opportunities to expand your skillset.
- Be open to feedback and actively seek out ways to improve yourself and your work.